Microwave Cook

Delicious, Easy & Quick Microwave Recipes

for People in a Hurry.

Author: Nicole Watson

Table of Contents

Microwave Cooking Fundamentals You Need To Know

If you think microwave cooking is simply a case of tossing a plate or container of food in the microwave and zapping it until it's hot, you're (happily) wrong! If you think this appliance is all about heating up mediocre pre-made meals from the supermarket, you're also wrong! Microwaves get a bad rap, but these appliances are actually enormously useful and you can make a whole range of healthy, delicious meals using them. From fish to fresh vegetables, and from jacket potatoes to cakes and brownies, there's almost nothing that you can't cook in the microwave if you make sure you know what you are doing. You can even scramble eggs in there! Snacks, starters, main meals, and desserts are all at your fingertips with this clever appliance, as long as you know how to use it correctly. So, how do you do that?

The most important thing to understand when you're cooking in the microwave is safety. There are a few safety rules that you must make sure you observe.

Safety

Firstly, let's look at containers. Containers must be labelled microwave-safe if you are going to use them. Most modern ceramics, like plates, cups, and bowls, are microwave-safe, but you should always check. Using unsafe containers could result in damage to both the container and the microwave. You must also make absolutely sure that you do not put any metal or metal-containing items in the microwave. That means no aluminium foil, no tins, no spoons, forks, knives, etc. If you aren't sure whether an item contains metal, don't heat it in your microwave. This poses a very significant fire risk. If you ever see anything sparking inside the microwave, turn the appliance off immediately. Styrofoam containers are also considered unsafe for use in the microwave, as are things like plastic bags and paper bags. These items can pose a fire risk. Only ever place a container that says microwave-safe in the appliance.

Furthermore, for safety reasons, always make sure that the item you are placing in the microwave can vent. If you are heating a Tupperware, pop the lid off. If you are cooking a food with a skin, such as a potato or a tomato, cut it open first. This will allow steam to escape. If you don't do this, there's a risk that the food will explode. Never place anything airtight in your microwave.

You should make sure you are always nearby when you are cooking anything in the microwave. A lot of people switch the appliance on and then walk away, but this isn't safe. You don't have to stare at it throughout the cooking time, but make sure you are available so you can step in your food cooks faster than expected, or anything else changes.

As a final safety precaution, remember that food coming out of the microwave is likely to be steaming, and the dishes will be hot. Check you are protecting your hands if necessary.

How To Heat Food Through

It's also important to understand the proper approach for heating food throughout. A lot of people have suffered the annoyance of getting a dish out of the microwave, only to find it's still cold in the centre, even though it's sizzling hot around the edges.

The heat of the microwave penetrates the food from the outer edge inward, up to 4 cm deep. Food that is in the centre of the dish (more than 4cm from the outside in any direction) will not be exposed to much heat, and will remain almost cold, only warming up as heat transfers inwards.

You therefore need to make sure you are stirring the food as it cooks to ensure the heat is distributed evenly. Allowing the food to stand for short periods while it is being heated is also important; this permits the heat to spread through the dish, and prevents parts from getting too hot, while other parts remain cold.

What Kinds Of Food Can You Cook?

You can cook many different foods in the microwave, but in general, moisture-based foods are the best. Meats and other foods that do not contain much moisture tend to get dried out in the microwave, and are more prone to burning. Things like soups, sauces, and stews work particularly well.

That said, you should experiment! This book will give you some great ideas, but feel free to look around for others, in case you find something that appeals. There are lots of amazing meals out there.

Secrets & Tips Of Microwave Cooking For Easy & Delicious Meals

Now you understand the fundamentals of making microwave meals, let's look at a few tips to ensure your cooking is as good as it can be!

Know Your Wattage

Microwaves vary significantly in terms of their wattage, and you need to make sure you understand how to adjust your cooking times accordingly. If you cook food in a low wattage microwave, it will take longer than in a high wattage microwave.

Some recipes will tell you how to adjust, but many are based on 850 watt appliances. To adjust, use the below table:

- 800 watts: add 5 seconds per 1 minute
- 750 watts: add 10 seconds per 1 minute
- 700 watts: add 15 seconds per 1 minute
- 650 watts: add 20 seconds per 1 minute

This will ensure your food is hot throughout, and not overcooked. For example, if the recipe says to cook the meal for 3 minutes in an 850 watt appliance, you would cook it for 3 minutes and 15 seconds in an 800 watt appliance.

Salt Later

A lot of people put salt on their meals before cooking them, but this is a bad idea when you're microwaving food. The salt crystals can attract the microwaves, and this prevents the heat from penetrating the food as effectively. It can also lead to the outer layer of food becoming dry.

You should therefore only add the salt when the food is cooked and you are ready to eat it. This will also let you adjust the amount of salt according to the food's final flavour.

Use Round Containers

Because the heat penetrates from all sides, round containers will offer the best heat distribution. Containers with corners can cause the food in the corners to overcook.

Spread Food Out

Since the heat can only penetrate about 4 cm deep, you should aim to spread the food out to decrease the cooking time and more evenly distribute the heat. Where possible, making a hollow in the centre of the food (e.g. spread fish pie out in a doughnut shape) will maximise the efficiency.

Cover Your Foods

Although you do need to make sure you let foods vent as described earlier, providing some cover can help to trap steam around the food, and this often makes it more tender and succulent.

Putting a loose-fitting lid or plate over the top of your dish while microwaving it is a good idea. Always check that steam can escape, however.

Skip The Oil

One of the things that makes microwave cooking healthier is that you do not need to grease the container, so you can massively reduce (or simply skip) the oil in many recipes. This is because microwaves create a moist cooking environment due to the steam, and the food is unlikely to stick to the containers.

Of course, you may still want to include oil for the sake of flavour and texture, but this is still a great way to reduce the amount of fat you use when cooking.

4 Common Mistakes You Must Avoid

Of course, there are a few major "don'ts when it comes to cooking in the microwave, so let's cover a few of those here.

1) Not Cleaning It Properly

Nobody wants to clean the microwave, but it's important to regularly do so. Baked-on food will reduce the appliance's efficiency, increase the cooking times, and could be a hygiene hazard if it is left for too long.

You can clean your microwave more easily by heating a cup of water in there to create steam. The steam will loosen any stuck food, making it easier to wipe it away.

2) Microwaving The Wrong Foods

The following foods will not cook well in the microwave, for various reasons. You need to avoid putting these foods, or any meals containing them, in your microwave.

- Hard-boiled eggs: the steam will build up inside the egg, as it cannot escape, and the egg will explode. This can be quite dangerous, as it often only occurs after you have removed the egg from the microwave, so you may get scalded.

- Chilli peppers: the heat of the microwave can release a lot of capsaicin, which is what gives them their hotness. This will vent into the air, and may result in stinging/burning eyes.

- Eggs in their shell: these will also explode, because the steam cannot vent and the egg cannot expand.

- Grapes: you might be surprised to find out that grapes can be another potential fire hazard. This is because they act as antennae, conducting electric currents, and this can result in sparks of plasma – which can start a fire.

- Frozen meat: defrosting large pieces of frozen meat is also considered unwise. This is because of the uneven heat distribution. If certain parts of the meat heat up faster than others, bacteria may begin growing in these parts, while other areas remain frozen. This poses food safety issues unless you cook the meat immediately. It's also very easy to dry meat out in the microwave if you cook it from frozen.

- Bread: bread isn't dangerous when heated in the microwave, but it quickly becomes very unappetising. This is because the sugar molecules in the starch melt when the bread is heated, and then recrystallise when the bread cools. The bread becomes chewy and hard. This is true of other flour-based products, such as pastries, bagels, etc. You cannot make toast in the microwave.

- Dry leafy greens: you can cook leafy greens in the microwave provided you add water to them. There are high concentrations of iron and magnesium in the greens, and if there's no water to spread the heat around, the greens may start to spark. If you heat a lot or leave them for too long, this could be a fire risk.

- Processed meat: these meats aren't considered healthy anyway, but some studies have indicated that microwaving processed meat results in higher production of cholesterol oxidation products (COPs). Opt for other methods of heating things like ham, hot dogs, etc.

3) Not Letting Food Rest

You might be keen to dig into your piping-hot dinner, but it's a good idea to give it a few minutes before you do so. The food will have pockets of heat in it at this point, and you may burn yourself. You should wait about 5 minutes so the heat can redistribute throughout.

4) Closing The Door When It's Wet Inside

If you shut the microwave door as soon as you've finished cooking, you may be shortening the lifespan of your appliance. It probably won't affect it for a while, but trapping all the steam in there constantly will eventually start to damage the inside of the microwave.

You may start to notice spots of rust appearing, and these are a sign that the microwave needs to be scrapped. As soon as it starts rusting, it becomes a fire risk, and either needs to be professionally repaired, or responsibly recycled.

You can prevent this from happening by letting the microwave dry out after it has been used. Remember, there's a lot of steam when you microwave food – so either leave the door open, or dry the interior with a clean, soft cloth. This should maximise the appliance's longevity.

Pumpkin Oatmeal

Servings | 2   Time | 12 minutes

Nutritional Content (per serving):

Cal | 223   Fat | 4.6g   Protein | 22.9g   Carbs | 28.7g   Fibre | 5.8g

Ingredients:

- ❖ 480 millilitres (2 cups) hot water
- ❖ 40 grams (1/3 cup) rolled oats
- ❖ 2½ grams (½ teaspoon) ground cinnamon
- ❖ 2 scoops unsweetened vanilla protein powder
- ❖ 85 grams (1/3 cup) pumpkin puree
- ❖ 20 grams (2 tablespoons) chia seeds
- ❖ 1¼ grams (¼ teaspoon) ground ginger
- ❖ 20 grams (1 tablespoon) maple syrup

Directions:

1. In a microwave-safe bowl, place water, pumpkin puree, oats, chia seeds and spices and mix well.
2. Microwave on "High" for about 2 minutes.
3. Remove the bowl of oatmeal from the microwave and stir in the protein powder and maple syrup.
4. Serve immediately.

Banana Oatmeal

Servings|1   Time|10 minutes
Nutritional Content (per serving):
Cal| 300   Fat| 6.1g   Protein| 8g   Carbs| 57.8g   Fibre| 9.2g

Ingredients:

- ❖ 240 millilitres (1 cup) water
- ❖ 1 banana, peeled and sliced
- ❖ 5 grams (1½ tablespoons) almonds, chopped

- ❖ 50 grams (½ cup) rolled oats
- ❖ 1¼ grams (¼ teaspoon) ground cinnamon

Directions:

1. Place the water and oats in a microwave-safe bowl and mix well.
2. Microwave on "High" for about 3 minutes.
3. Transfer the oat mixture into a serving bowl and stir in banana slices and cinnamon.
4. Top with almonds and serve.

Seeds & Coconut Porridge

Servings | 1   Time | 10 minutes
Nutritional Content (per serving):
Cal| 301   Fat| 23.7g   Protein| 12.8g   Carbs| 11.8g   Fibre| 8.8g

Ingredients:

- 120 millilitres (½ cup) water
- 15 grams (2 tablespoons) almond flour
- 10 grams (1 tablespoon) golden flaxseed meal
- 5 grams (1 teaspoon) granulated sugar
- 2½ millilitres (½ teaspoon) vanilla extract
- 20 grams (2 tablespoons) hemp hearts
- 15 grams (2 tablespoons) unsweetened coconut, shredded
- 10 grams (1 tablespoon) chia seeds
- Pinch of salt

Directions:

1. In a large microwave-safe bowl, add all the ingredients except the vanilla extract and microwave on "High" for about 2 minutes or until thickened.
2. Remove from the microwave and stir in the vanilla extract.
3. Serve warm.

Oats Granola

Servings|1   Time|10 minutes
Nutritional Content (per serving):
Cal| 304   Fat| 8.4g   Protein| 4.1g   Carbs| 32.9g   Fibre| 3.4g

Ingredients:

- ❖ 30 grams (4½ tablespoons) rolled oats
- ❖ 10 grams (1 tablespoon) pecans, chopped
- ❖ 10 millilitres (2 teaspoons) water
- ❖ Pinch of salt

- ❖ 5 grams (1 tablespoon) desiccated coconut
- ❖ 20 grams (1 tablespoon) maple syrup
- ❖ 10 millilitres (2 teaspoons) vegetable oil

Directions:

1. In a large microwave-safe mug, add oats and remaining ingredients and mix well.
2. Microwave on "High" for about 2½ minutes, stirring once after 1½ minutes.
3. Remove the owl from microwave and set aside for about 2-3 minutes before serving.

Simple Bread

Servings|2   Time|10 minutes
Nutritional Content (per serving):
Cal| 317   Fat| 28.1g   Protein| 6.8g   Carbs| 11.5g   Fibre| 2g

Ingredients:

- ❖ Non-stick cooking spray
- ❖ 2 grams (2½ grams (½ teaspoon) baking powder
- ❖ 30 grams (2½ tablespoons) coconut oil, softened

- ❖ 40 grams (1/3 cup) almond flour
- ❖ Pinch of salt
- ❖ 1 egg
- ❖ 20 grams (1 tablespoon) maple syrup

Directions:

1. Grease a microwave-safe mug with cooking spray.
2. In a bowl, mix together flour, baking powder and salt.
3. In another small bowl, add oil and egg and beat well.
4. Add the egg mixture into the flour mixture and mix until just combined.
5. Transfer the mixture into prepared mug.
6. Microwave on "High" for about 1½ minutes.
7. Remove from microwave and let it cool for about 5 minutes.
8. Carefully remove from mug and cut into 2 equal-sized slices.
9. Drizzle with maple syrup and serve.

Cheddar Bread

Servings|1   Time|10 minutes
Nutritional Content (per serving):
Cal| 282   Fat| 22.7g   Protein| 16.3g   Carbs| 5.6g   Fibre| 4g

Ingredients:

- ❖ 5 grams (1 teaspoon) butter, melted
- ❖ 1 package Splenda
- ❖ 30 grams (¼ cup) cheddar cheese, shredded
- ❖ 1 large egg
- ❖ 20 grams (2 tablespoons) flaxseed meal
- ❖ 2 grams (2½ grams (½ teaspoon) baking powder

Directions:

1. Coat a microwave-safe mug with melted butter.
2. In a bowl, add remaining ingredients and mix well.
3. Transfer the mixture into the prepared mug.
4. Microwave on "High" for about 1-1¼ minutes.
5. Serve warm.

Cornbread Muffin

Servings|1 Time|10 minutes
Nutritional Content (per serving):
Cal| 185   Fat| 8.5g   Protein| 3g   Carbs| 25.2g   Fibre| 1g

Ingredients:

- ❖ Non-stick cooking spray
- ❖ 10 grams (1 tablespoon) yellow cornmeal
- ❖ 10 grams (2 teaspoons) butter, melted
- ❖ 20 millilitres (4 teaspoons) milk

- ❖ 15 grams (2 tablespoons) all-purpose flour
- ❖ 1¼ grams (¼ teaspoon) baking powder
- ❖ 5 grams (1 teaspoon) honey

Directions:

1. Grease a microwave-safe mug with cooking spray.
2. In a small bowl, mix together the flour, cornmeal, and baking powder.
3. Add the butter, honey and milk and mix until well combined.
4. Place the mixture into the prepared mug.
5. Microwave on "High" for about 50-60 seconds.
6. Serve warm.

Egg Puff

Servings|1   Time|10 minutes
Nutritional Content (per serving):
Cal| 376   Fat| 28.6g   Protein| 15.4g   Carbs| 15.6g   Fibre| 0g

Ingredients:

- ❖ 55 grams (2 ounces) cream cheese, softened
- ❖ 1-2 drops liquid stevia
- ❖ 2 eggs
- ❖ 20 grams (1 tablespoon) maple syrup

Directions:

1. In a microwave-safe bowl, add all ingredients and stir to combine well.
2. Microwave on "High" for about 45 seconds.
3. Remove from microwave and stir again.
4. Microwave on "High" for about 2 minutes.
5. Serve immediately.

Ham & Courgette Frittata

Servings | 4   Time | 25 minutes
Nutritional Content (per serving):
Cal | 271   Fat | 17.5g   Protein | 20.9g   Carbs | 8.6g   Fibre | 2.4g

Ingredients:

- ❖ 3 medium courgettes, finely chopped
- ❖ 4 large eggs
- ❖ 115 grams (1 cup) cheddar cheese, shredded
- ❖ 1 small onion, chopped
- ❖ Salt and ground black pepper, as required
- ❖ 135 grams (1 cup) cooked ham, cubed

Directions:

1. In a 9-inch microwave-safe pie plate, blend together the courgette and onion.
2. With plastic wrap, cover the pie plate and microwave on "High" for about 3-4 minutes.
3. In a bowl, add eggs, salt and black pepper and beat until well combined.
4. Add the ham and cheese and stir to combine.
5. Remove the pie plate and drain any liquid.
6. Place the egg mixture over courgette mixture and microwave on "70% power" for about 8-9 minutes.
7. Serve warm.

Bacon

Servings | 2   Time | 5 minutes
Nutritional Content (per serving):
Cal | 290   Fat | 24.9g   Protein | 16.6g   Carbs | 0g   Fibre | 0g

Ingredients:

❖ 4 medium-thick bacon slices

Directions:

1. Arrange two paper towels onto a microwave-safe plate.
2. Arrange 4 bacon slices over the paper towels, leaving space between each other.
3. Arrange 2 paper towels on top of bacon slices.
4. Microwave on "High" or about 4 minutes.
5. Serve hot.

Chicken & Rice Soup

Servings|1   Time|15 minutes
Nutritional Content (per serving):
Cal| 300   Fat| 4.5g   Protein| 42.8g   Carbs| 18.7g   Fibre| 0.4g

Ingredients:

- ❖ 25 grams (2 tablespoons) uncooked instant rice
- ❖ 5 grams (1 teaspoon) dried celery flakes
- ❖ 1¼ grams (¼ teaspoon) dried minced onion
- ❖ 360 millilitres (¾ cup) boiling water
- ❖ 5 grams (1 teaspoon) chicken bouillon granules
- ❖ 5 grams (1 teaspoon) dried parsley flakes
- ❖ Salt and ground black pepper, as required
- ❖ 1 (140-gram) (5-ounce) can chunk white chicken, drained

Directions:

1. In a small bowl, combine the rice, chicken bouillon granules, celery flakes, parsley flakes, minced onion, salt and black pepper and mix well.
2. In a microwave-safe bowl, place rice mixture and top with boiling water.
3. Immediately cover the bowl for about 5 minutes.
4. Uncover the bowl and stir in the chicken.
5. Microwave on "High" for about 1-2 minutes.
6. Serve immediately.

Tomato Soup

Servings|4   Time|30 minutes

Nutritional Content (per serving):

Cal| 33   Fat| 0.2g   Protein| 1.2g   Carbs| 7.5g   Fibre| 1.8g

Ingredients:

- ❖ 3 tomatoes, finely chopped
- ❖ 5 grams (1 teaspoon) fresh ginger, sliced
- ❖ Water, as required

- ❖ 1 onion, finely chopped
- ❖ 5 grams (1 teaspoon) white sugar
- ❖ Salt and ground black pepper, as required

Directions:

1. Place the tomato, onion and ginger in a microwave-safe bowl and mix.
2. Cover the bowl and microwave on "High" for about 8 minutes, stirring twice.
3. Remove from the microwave and discard the ginger slices.
4. Place the tomato mixture in a blender and pulse until smooth.
5. Through a fine mesh strainer, strain the mixture.
6. Add the sugar and a little water and stir to combine.
7. Return the soup into the same bowl and microwave on "High" for about 7 minutes, stirring twice.
8. Remove from the microwave and stir in the salt and black pepper.
9. Serve hot.

Bacon & Potato Soup

Servings | 1   Time | 20 minutes
Nutritional Content (per serving):
Cal | 183   Fat | 9.8g   Protein | 9.4g   Carbs | 14.4g   Fibre | 0.9g

Ingredients:

- 180 millilitres (¾ cup) water
- 10 grams (1 tablespoon) onion, chopped
- 1 cooked bacon slice, chopped
- 10 grams (2 teaspoons) cornstarch
- Salt and ground black pepper, as required
- 60 millilitres (¼ cup) milk
- 25 grams (3 tablespoons) potatoes, cut into small cubes
- 15 grams (2 tablespoons) cheddar cheese, shredded
- 120 millilitres (½ cup) chicken broth
- 15 grams (1 tablespoon) sour cream

Directions:

1. In a large microwave-safe mug, place potatoes and water and microwave on "High" for about 3-4 minutes.
2. Remove the bowl from microwave and drain the water.
3. In the bowl of potatoes, add the onion, bacon, cheese, cornstarch, salt and pepper and mix until well combined.
4. Add the broth and milk and stir to combine.
5. Microwave on "High" for about 2½-3 minutes.
6. Serve hot with the topping of sour cream.

Herbed Veggie Soup

Servings│4   Time│20 minutes
Nutritional Content (per serving):
Cal│ 154   Fat│ 13g   Protein│ 3.1g   Carbs│ 9.2g   Fibre│ 5.1g

Ingredients:

- 35 grams (¼ cup) whole almonds, soaked overnight and drained
- 60 grams (2 cups) fresh spinach
- 2 celery stalks, chopped
- 15 grams (2 tablespoons) onion, chopped
- 1 garlic clove, chopped
- 10 grams (¼ cup) fresh parsley leaves
- Salt and ground black pepper, as required
- 360 millilitres (1½ cups) water
- 1 large avocado, peeled, pitted and chopped
- 1 small courgette, chopped
- ½ small green capsicum, seeded and chopped
- 10 grams (¼ cup) fresh coriander leaves
- 30 millilitres (2 tablespoons fresh lemon juice

Directions:

1. Add all the ingredients in a high-speed blender and pulse until smooth.
2. Transfer the soup into a large microwave-safe bowl and microwave on "High" for about 2-3 minutes or until just warmed.
3. Serve immediately.

Black Beans & Corn Soup

Servings|3   Time|15 minutes
Nutritional Content (per serving):
Cal| 195   Fat| 1.4g   Protein| 9.2g   Carbs| 39.5g   Fibre| 9.2g

Ingredients:

- 100 grams (7 ounces) canned fire-roasted tomatoes
- 65 grams (½ cup) frozen corn, thawed
- 180 millilitres (¾ cup) water
- 1¼ grams (¼ teaspoon) ground cumin
- 1 corn tortilla, thinly sliced
- 130 grams (½ cup) salsa
- 100 grams (7 ounces) canned black beans, rinsed and drained
- 1¼ grams (¼ teaspoon) red chili powder
- Pinch of cayenne powder
- 5 millilitres (1 teaspoon) fresh lime juice

Directions:

1. In a microwave-safe bowl, add all the ingredients except for the lime juice and mix well.
2. Microwave on "High" for about 2-3 minutes, stirring twice.
3. Serve hot with the drizzling of lime juice.

Ketchup-Glazed Chicken Drumsticks

Servings|8   Time|25 minutes
Nutritional Content (per serving):
Cal| 327   Fat| 10.3g   Protein| 47.7g   Carbs| 9.4g   Fibre| 1.2g

Ingredients:

- ❖ 300 grams (1 cup) ketchup
- ❖ 5 grams (1 teaspoon) cayenne powder
- ❖ 60 grams (¼ cup) curry powder
- ❖ 8 chicken drumsticks

Directions:

1. In a large, microwave-safe dish, blend together the ketchup, cayenne pepper and curry.
2. Add the chicken drumsticks and coat with ketchup mixture generously.
3. Arrange the chicken drumsticks in a circle, with the thin part in the center of dish.
4. Cover the casserole dish and microwave on "High" for about 12-15 minutes.
5. Serve hot.

Crispy Chicken Thighs

Servings|8   Time|30 minutes
Nutritional Content (per serving):
Cal| 255   Fat| 9.8g   Protein| 33.7g   Carbs| 6.9g   Fibre| 0.5g

Ingredients:

❖ 65 grams (½ cup) Bisquick mix
❖ 10 grams (2 teaspoons) red chili powder
❖ 8 (115-grams) (4-ounce) chicken thighs

❖ 20 grams (2 tablespoons) yellow cornmeal
❖ 5 grams (1 teaspoon) paprika
❖ Salt and ground black pepper, as required

Directions:

1. In a large bowl, blend together the Bisquick mix, cornmeal, chili powder, paprika, salt and black pepper.
2. Add the chicken thighs and toss to coat well.
3. In a 9-inch microwave-safe pie plate, arrange the chicken thighs, skin sides up.
4. With waxed paper, cover the pie plate and microwave on "High" for about 10 minutes.
5. Rotate the pie plate and microwave on "High" for about 6-9 minutes.
6. Serve hot.

Chicken Parmesan

Servings | 2   Time | 10 minutes
Nutritional Content (per serving):
Cal | 298   Fat | 12.7g   Protein | 39.4g   Carbs | 5.5g   Fibre | 2.7g

Ingredients:

- ❖ 1 (225-gram) (8-ounce) can tomato sauce
- ❖ 1¼ grams (¼ teaspoon) garlic powder
- ❖ 40 grams (½ cup) cornflake, crushed
- ❖ 5 grams (1 teaspoon) dried parsley flakes, crushed
- ❖ 85 grams (¾ cup) mozzarella cheese, shredded

- ❖ 5 grams (1 teaspoon) Italian seasoning
- ❖ 1 egg, beaten
- ❖ 30 grams (¼ cup) Parmesan cheese, grated
- ❖ 6 (115-grams) (4-ounce) boneless, skinless chicken breast halves
- ❖ Non-stick cooking spray

Directions:

1. In a microwave-safe bowl, blend together the tomato sauce, Italian seasoning and garlic powder.
2. Cover the bowl and microwave on "High" for about 2 minutes.
3. Stir the mixture and microwave on 50% power" for about 3-5 minutes, stirring once halfway through.
4. Remove the bow from microwave and set aside.
5. In a shallow bowl, place the egg.
6. In another shallow bowl, add the cornflake crumbs, Parmesan cheese and parsley and mix well.
7. Dip the chicken into beaten egg and then coat with Parmesan mixture.
8. Lightly grease a shallow, microwave-safe dish with cooking spray.
9. Arrange the chicken thighs into the prepared dish in a single layer.
10. Cover the dish and microwave on "High" for about 10-12 minutes, rotating the dish once after 5 minutes.
11. Place the tomato sauce mixture over the chicken thighs and sprinkle with mozzarella cheese evenly.
12. Microwave, uncovered on "50% power" for about 3-5 minutes.
13. Serve hot.

Chicken Cordon Bleu

Servings|6   Time|30 minutes
Nutritional Content (per serving):
Cal| 396   Fat| 20.2g   Protein| 44g   Carbs| 8.7g   Fibre| 1.9g

Ingredients:

- 40 grams (2 tablespoons) butter, cubed
- 6 (115-grams) (4-ounce) boneless skinless chicken breast halves
- 20 grams (1/3 cup) fresh mushrooms, sliced
- 5 grams (1 teaspoon) dried oregano
- 2½ grams (½ teaspoon) garlic powder
- 2½ grams (½ teaspoon) salt
- 6 Swiss cheese slices

- 2½ grams (½ teaspoon) dried sage, crushed
- 1 medium capsicum, seeded and julienned
- 1 (425-gram) (15-ounce) can tomato sauce
- 5 grams (1 teaspoon) white sugar
- 2½ grams (½ teaspoon) lemon-pepper seasoning
- 6 deli ham slices

Directions:

1. In a microwave-safe dish, place butter and sage and microwave on "High" for about 30 seconds.
2. Remove from microwave and coat the chicken breasts with butter mixture evenly.
3. Now, arrange the chicken breasts in a single layer.
4. Spread capsicum and mushrooms on top of chicken breasts.
5. Microwave on "High" for about 8-10 minutes, flipping twice.
6. With a slotted spoon, transfer the chicken breasts and vegetables onto a plate.
7. With a piece of foil, cover the plate of chicken mixture to keep warm.
8. In the dish, add the tomato sauce, sugar, oregano, spices and salt and mix with the cooking juices.
9. Microwave on "High" for about 2 minutes.
10. Arrange the chicken breasts into the dish and top with ham, followed by cheese, cooked mushroom and capsicum.
11. Cook on "High" for about 2 minutes.
12. Serve hot.

Chicken Kiev

Servings | 4   Time | 20 minutes

Nutritional Content (per serving):

Cal | 465   Fat | 27.3g   Protein | 50.1g   Carbs | 2.3g   Fibre | 0.2g

Ingredients:

- ❖ 60 grams (3 tablespoons) butter, softened
- ❖ 1¼ grams (¼ teaspoon) garlic powder
- ❖ 4 (150-gram) (6-ounce) boneless, skinless chicken breasts, pounded slightly
- ❖ 30 grams (1/3 cup) cornflake, crushed
- ❖ 2½ grams (½ teaspoon) dried parsley
- ❖ 1¼ grams (¼ teaspoon) paprika
- ❖ 5 grams (1 teaspoon) fresh chives, minced
- ❖ 1¼ grams (¼ teaspoon) ground white pepper
- ❖ 40 grams (2 tablespoons) butter, melted
- ❖ 10 grams (1 tablespoon) Parmesan cheese, grated

Directions:

1. In a small bowl, add softened butter, chives, garlic powder and white pepper and mix well.
2. Divide the butter mixture into four cubes.
3. With plastic wrap, cover the butter cubes and freeze for about 10 minutes.
4. Arrange the chicken breasts onto a smooth surface.
5. Place 1 butter cube in the center of each chicken breast.
6. Fold each chicken breast over butter cube and then secure with a toothpick.
7. In a shallow bowl, place the melted butter.
8. In another shallow bowl, add the cornflakes, cheese, parsley and paprika and mix well.
9. Dip each chicken breast into melted butter and then coat with cornflake mixture.
10. In a microwave-safe dish, arrange the chicken breasts, seam side down.
11. Microwave on "High" for about 5-6 minutes.
12. Serve hot.

Chicken with Mushrooms

Servings|4   Time|35 minutes
Nutritional Content (per serving):
Cal| 414   Fat| 23.1g   Protein| 38.2g   Carbs| 15.3g   Fibre| 2.4g

Ingredients:

- 455 grams (1 pound) boneless chicken breasts, chopped
- 100 grams (3½ ounces) sweetcorn
- 4 garlic cloves, minced
- 60 millilitres (¼ cup) olive oil
- 10 grams (2 teaspoons) paprika
- Salt and ground black pepper, as required
- 200 grams (7 ounces) fresh mushrooms, sliced
- ½ large onion, chopped
- 240 millilitres (1 cup) milk
- 15 millilitres (1 tablespoon) fresh lemon juice

Directions:

1. In a shallow, microwave-safe dish, add chicken cubes and remaining ingredient and mix until well combined.
2. With a lid, cover the dish and microwave on "High" for about 20 minutes.
3. Remove from microwave and stir the mixture well.
4. Set aside for about 5 minutes before serving.

Steak in Olives Sauce

Servings|4   Time|1 hour 5 minutes
Nutritional Content (per serving):
Cal| 428   Fat| 21.9g   Protein| 43.5g   Carbs| 13.1g   Fibre| 4.4g

Ingredients:

- 30 millilitres (2 tablespoons) olive oil
- 3 garlic cloves, minced
- 2½ grams (½ teaspoon) ground cumin
- 1 (400-gram) (14-ounce) can crushed tomatoes
- 240 millilitres (1 cup) beef broth
- 1 bay leaf
- 5 grams (2 tablespoons) fresh coriander leaves, chopped
- 1 small onion, thinly sliced
- 1¼ grams (¼ teaspoon) dried oregano
- Salt and ground black pepper, as required
- 75 grams (½ cup) jarred roasted red peppers, sliced
- 10 millilitres (2 teaspoons) soy sauce
- 570 grams (1¼ pounds) flank steak, cut into thin strips
- 70 grams (1/3 cup) olives, halved

Directions:

1. In a large microwave-safe bowl, add oil, onion, garlic, oregano, cumin, oil, salt and black pepper and toss to coat well.
2. With plastic wrap, cover the bowl tightly.
3. With the tip of a paring knife, cut a small slit in the center of plastic wrap.
4. Microwave on "High" for about 4 minutes.
5. Uncover the bowl and stir in the tomatoes, red peppers, broth, soy sauce, bay leaf, salt and black pepper until well combined.
6. Add the steak slices and gently push into the broth mixture.
7. With 2 pieces of plastic wrap, cover the bowl tightly.
8. With the tip of a paring knife, cut a small slit in the center of plastic wrap.
9. Microwave on "High" for about 40 minutes, stirring once halfway through.
10. Remove the bowl from microwave and uncover it.
11. Set aside for about 5 minutes.
12. With a slotted spoon, transfer the steak slices onto a cutting board.
13. With two forks, shred the steak and return into the bowl.
14. Add the olives and stir to combine.
15. With plastic wrap, cover the bowl tightly.
16. With the tip of a paring knife, cut a small slit in the center of plastic wrap.
17. Microwave on "High" for about 5 minutes.
18. Remove the bowl from microwave and set aside, covered for about 5 minutes.
19. Stir in the coriander and serve.

Stuffed Capsicums

Servings | 4   Time | 30 minutes
Nutritional Content (per serving):
Cal | 282   Fat | 7.2g   Protein | 23.2g   Carbs | 31.2g   Fibre | 2.9g

Ingredients:

- ❖ 4 large capsicums
- ❖ 95 grams (½ cup) cooked rice
- ❖ 15 grams (2 tablespoons) onions, chopped
- ❖ Salt and ground black pepper, as required
- ❖ 225 grams (½ pound) cooked ground beef
- ❖ 1 (225-gram) (8-ounce) can tomato sauce
- ❖ Pinch of garlic salt
- ❖ 45 grams (1/3 cup) cheddar cheese, grated

Directions:

1. Cut off the top of each pepper and then remove the seeds and membranes.
2. In a microwave-safe dish, arrange the capsicums, cut-side down.
3. With a plastic wrap, cover the baking dish and microwave on "High" for about 3-3½ minutes.
4. Meanwhile, in a bowl, add ground beef, rice, tomato sauce, onions, salt, and 1/8 teaspoon garlic salt and mix well.
5. Remove from microwave and uncover the dish.
6. Stuff each capsicum with beef mixture evenly.
7. With a plastic wrap, cover the baking dish and microwave on "High" for about 10 minutes.
8. Remove the dish of capsicums from microwave and sprinkle each with cheese evenly.
9. Again, cover the dish and microwave on "High" for about 2-3 minutes.
10. Serve warm.

Meatballs in Sauce

Servings | 8   Time | 20 minutes
Nutritional Content (per serving):
Cal | 485   Fat | 23g   Protein | 19.6g   Carbs | 49.8g   Fibre | 2.3g

Ingredients:

- 1 (285-gram) (10-ounce) jar sweet and sour sauce
- 2 medium carrots, peeled and julienned
- 1 small green capsicum, seeded and julienned
- 25 millilitres (4½ teaspoons) soy sauce
- 910 grams (2 pounds) frozen fully-cooked meatballs, thawed
- 1 small onion, sliced
- 1 garlic clove, minced

Directions:

1. In a small bowl, blend together the sweet and sour sauce and soy sauce.
2. In large microwave-safe dish, place the meatballs in a single layer.
3. Arrange the carrots, capsicum, onion and garlic over meatballs and top with sauce mixture evenly.
4. Cover the dish and microwave on "High" for about 6-8 minutes, stirring twice.
5. Serve hot.

Pork Meatloaf

Servings | 6   Time | 30 minutes
Nutritional Content (per serving):
Cal | 265   Fat | 12.9g   Protein | 15.6g   Carbs | 22.6g   Fibre | 0.6g

Ingredients:

- ❖ 1 large egg, lightly beaten
- ❖ 75 grams (½ cup) dry breadcrumbs
- ❖ 40 grams (2 tablespoons) prepared mustard
- ❖ 455 grams (1 pound) lean ground pork
- ❖ 30 millilitres (2 tablespoons) apple cider vinegar

- ❖ 30 grams (2 tablespoons) onion soup mix
- ❖ 100 grams (5 tablespoons) ketchup, divided
- ❖ Salt and ground black pepper, as required
- ❖ 80 grams (¼ cup) white sugar
- ❖ 20 grams (2 tablespoons) brown sugar

Directions:

1. In a large bowl, add egg, 40 grams (2 tablespoons) of ketchup, breadcrumbs, dry soup mix, mustard, salt and pepper and mix until well combined.
2. Add in the ground pork and mix well.
3. Shape the beef mixture into an oval loaf.
4. Arrange the loaf in a shallow, microwave-safe dish.
5. Cover the dish and microwave on "High" for about 10-12 minutes.
6. Remove the dish from microwave and carefully drain any liquid.
7. In a small bowl, add remaining ketchup, sugars and vinegar and mix well.
8. Spread ketchup mixture over meatloaf evenly.
9. Cover the dish and microwave on "High" for about 2-3 minutes.
10. Remove the dish of meatloaf from microwave and set aside for about 10 minutes before serving.
11. Cut into desired-sized slices and serve.

Herbed Courgette Meatloaf

Servings|6   Time|45 minutes
Nutritional Content (per serving):
Cal| 243   Fat| 12g   Protein| 24g   Carbs| 7g   Fibre| 2g

Ingredients:

- ❖ Non-stick cooking spray
- ❖ 225 grams (½ pound) ground turkey
- ❖ 60 grams (½ cup) courgette, shredded
- ❖ 5 grams (1 teaspoon) bottled minced garlic, divided
- ❖ 5 grams (1 teaspoon) dried thyme, crushed
- ❖ Salt and ground black pepper, as required
- ❖ 455 grams (1 pound) lean ground beef
- ❖ 25 grams (¼ cup) rolled oats
- ❖ 30 grams (¼ cup) onion, finely chopped
- ❖ 10 grams (3 tablespoons) fresh parsley, chopped and divided
- ❖ 1 (225-gram) (8-ounce) jar pizza sauce, divided

Directions:

1. Grease a microwave-safe pie plate with cooking spray.
2. In a large bowl, add turkey, beef, oats, courgette, onion, 2½ grams (½ teaspoon) of garlic, 2 tablespoons of parsley, thyme, salt, black pepper and 40 grams (2 tablespoons) of pizza sauce and mix until well combined.
3. Shape the mixture into a loaf.
4. Arrange the meatloaf onto the prepared pie plate.
5. With a large parchment paper, cover the pie plate.
6. Microwave on "High" for about 5 minutes, flipping once halfway through.
7. Remove from microwave and remove the drippings.
8. In a bowl, mix together remaining garlic, parsley and pizza sauce.
9. Spread sauce mixture over meatloaf evenly.
10. Again, cover the pie plate with parchment paper.
11. Now, set microwave on "50% power" for about 21-24 minutes, rotating the plate twice.
12. Remove from microwave and set aside for about 5 minutes before serving.
13. Cut into desired-sized slices and serve.

Pepperoni Pizza

Servings | 1   Time | 10 minutes
Nutritional Content (per serving):
Cal | 701   Fat | 50.7g   Protein | 28g   Carbs | 29.6g   Fibre | 1.3g

Ingredients:

- 35 grams (¼ cup) all-purpose flour
- ¼ gram (1/16 teaspoon) baking soda
- 45 millilitres (3 tablespoons) milk
- 20 grams (1 tablespoon) marinara sauce
- 5 mini pepperoni slices
- 1¼ grams (¼ teaspoon) dried basil
- ½ gram (1/8 teaspoon) baking powder
- ½ gram (1/8 teaspoon) salt
- 15 millilitres (1 tablespoon) olive oil
- 10 grams (1 tablespoon) mozzarella cheese, shredded

Directions:

1. In a microwave-safe mug, blend together the flour, baking powder, baking soda and salt.
2. Add the milk and oil and mix until well combined.
3. With a spoon, smooth the flour mixture and top with marinara sauce evenly.
4. Sprinkle with mozzarella cheese, followed by pepperoni and basil.
5. Microwave on "High" for about 70-80 seconds.
6. Serve hot.

Spiced Salmon

Servings|4   Time|15 minutes
Nutritional Content (per serving):
Cal| 153   Fat| 7.1g   Protein| 22.2g   Carbs| 0.5g   Fibre| 0.2g

Ingredients:

- ❖ 2½ grams (½ teaspoon) dried parsley
- ❖ ½ grams (½ teaspoon) paprika
- ❖ Salt, as required

- ❖ 2½ grams (½ teaspoon) ground cumin
- ❖ 2½ grams (½ teaspoon) garlic powder
- ❖ 4 (115-grams) (4-ounce) salmon fillets

Directions:

1. In a small bowl, blend together the parsley, spices and salt.
2. Coat the salmon fillets with spice mixture generously.
3. Refrigerate for about ½ hour.
4. Arrange the salmon fillets onto a microwave-safe dish and microwave on "High" for about 8-9 minutes.
5. Serve hot.

Vinegar Tilapia

Servings|4   Time|15 minutes
Nutritional Content (per serving):
Cal| 144   Fat| 4.4g   Protein| 23.4g   Carbs| 0.4g   Fibre| 0g

Ingredients:

- ❖ 4 (115-grams) (4-ounce) tilapia fillets
- ❖ 20 grams (1 tablespoon) chilled butter, chopped
- ❖ 30 millilitres (2 tablespoons) apple cider vinegar
- ❖ 1 garlic clove, minced
- ❖ 5 grams (1 tablespoon) fresh tarragon, finely chopped

Directions:

1. In a microwave-safe bowl, place tilapia fillets in a single layer.
2. Place garlic and then butter over each fillet at many places.
3. Top with tarragon evenly.
4. Cover the dish with a wax paper and broil for about 2 minutes per side.
5. Remove from microwave and uncover the dish.
6. Immediately, drizzle with vinegar and serve.

Lemony Cod

Servings|4   Time|15 minutes
Nutritional Content (per serving):
Cal| 164   Fat| 8.1g   Protein| 20.7g   Carbs| 2.1g   Fibre| 1.1g

Ingredients:

- 1 small tomato, chopped
- 1 garlic clove, minced
- 30 millilitres (2 tablespoons) water
- 30 millilitres (2 tablespoons) canola oil
- 2½ grams (½ teaspoon) dried basil
- 4 (115-grams) (4-ounce) cod fillets
- ½ small onion, finely chopped
- 30 millilitres (2 tablespoons) fresh lemon juice
- 5 grams (1 teaspoon) dried parsley
- Salt, as required
- 5 grams (1 teaspoon) seafood seasoning

Directions:

1. In a medium bowl, add tomato, onion, garlic, lemon juice, water, oil, dried herbs and salt and mix well.
2. In a microwave-safe dish, place the cod fillets in a single layer and top with tomato mixture.
3. Sprinkle with seafood seasoning evenly.
4. Cover the dish and microwave on "High" for about 5-6 minutes.
5. Serve hot.

Open-Faced Veggies Sandwich

Servings|4   Time|20 minutes
Nutritional Content (per serving):
Cal| 151   Fat| 11.5g   Protein| 1.9g   Carbs| 11.7g   Fibre| 1.6g

Ingredients:

- 30 millilitres (2 tablespoons) canola oil
- 75 grams (½ cup) capsicum, seeded and finely chopped
- ¼ of green chili, finely chopped
- 65 grams (½ cup) canned sweet corn kernels, rinsed and drained
- 5 grams (2 tablespoons) fresh coriander, chopped
- 20 grams (4 teaspoons) butter, softened
- 60 grams (½ cup) onion, finely chopped
- ¼ of green chili, finely chopped
- 75 grams (½ cup) capsicum, seeded and finely chopped
- 100 grams (½ cup) tomatoes, finely chopped
- Salt, as required
- 4 bread slices

Directions:

1. In a microwave-safe bowl, add the oil and microwave for about 30 seconds.
2. Add the onion and microwave for about 2 minutes, stirring once halfway through.
3. Stir in the capsicum and green chili and microwave for about 2 minutes, stirring once halfway through.
4. Stir in the corn, tomato, coriander and salt and microwave for about 2 minutes, stirring once halfway through.
5. Arrange the bread slices onto serving plates.
6. Spread the butter over each bread slice evenly and top with veggie mixture.
7. Cut each bread slice in 2 pieces and serve.

Soy Sauce Courgette Noodles

Servings | 2   Time | 20 minutes
Nutritional Content (per serving):
Cal | 59   Fat | 3.8g   Protein | 2.5g   Carbs | 6.1g   Fibre | 1.9g

Ingredients:

- ❖ 10 millilitres (2 teaspoons) olive oil
- ❖ Ground black pepper, as required
- ❖ 5 grams (1 tablespoon) fresh parsley, chopped

- ❖ 1 large courgette, spiralized with Blade C
- ❖ 15 millilitres (1 tablespoon) soy sauce

Directions:

1. Place the courgette noodles onto a microwave-safe plate and sprinkle with salt and black pepper.
2. Microwave on "High" for about 1 minute.
3. Drizzle with the oil and soy sauce and microwave for about 1 minute more.
4. Transfer courgette in a large serving plate and serve with the garnishing of parsley.

Potato Curry

Servings | 2   Time | 20 minutes
Nutritional Content (per serving):
Cal | 365   Fat | 35.7g   Protein | 3.7g   Carbs | 13.6g   Fibre | 3.6g

Ingredients:

- 105 grams (¾ cup) potato, finely chopped
- 180 millilitres (½ cup plus 2 tablespoons) water, divided
- 240 millilitres (1 cup) unsweetened coconut milk
- 5 grams (1 tablespoon) fresh coriander, chopped
- 10 grams (1 tablespoon) sweet corn kernels
- 15 millilitres (1 tablespoon) olive oil
- 25 grams (3 tablespoons) onion, chopped
- 10 grams (1 tablespoon) arrowroot flour
- 5 grams (1 teaspoon) curry powder
- Salt and ground black pepper, as required

Directions:

1. In a microwave-safe shallow dish, place the potato, corn and 120 millilitres (½ cup) of water and mix well.
2. Microwave on "High" for about 6 minutes.
3. Remove from the microwave and set aside.
4. In a microwave-safe bowl, place the oil and microwave on "High" for about 10-15 seconds.
5. In the bowl, add the onion and microwave on "High" for about 1 minute, stirring once halfway through.
6. Remove the bowl from microwave and stir in the cooked potato mixture and remaining water.
7. Microwave on "High" for about 1 minute.
8. Meanwhile, place the milk and flour in a bowl and mix well.
9. Remove the bowl from the microwave and stir in the flour mixture until well combined.
10. Microwave on "High" for about 4 minutes, stirring after every 1½ minutes.
11. Remove the bowl from microwave and stir in the salt and black pepper.
12. Serve hot with the garnishing of coriander.

Egg Fried Rice

Servings|2   Time|25 minutes
Nutritional Content (per serving):
Cal| 255   Fat| 6.1g   Protein| 7.2g   Carbs| 42g   Fibre| 3.1g

Ingredients:

- ❖ 5 millilitres (1 teaspoon) olive oil
- ❖ 90 grams (½ cup) basmati rice, soaked for 20 minutes and drained
- ❖ 240 millilitres (1 cup) water
- ❖ 2½ millilitres (½ teaspoon) sesame oil

- ❖ 1 egg, lightly whisked
- ❖ 90 grams (½ cup) mixed vegetables (carrots, capsicums and green peas)
- ❖ 5 millilitres (1 teaspoon) soy sauce
- ❖ ½ green onion, chopped

Directions:

1. In a microwave-safe bowl, place the oil and egg and microwave for about 1 minute.
2. Remove the bowl from microwave and with a fork, break the egg into small pieces.
3. Transfer the egg into a bowl. Set aside.
4. In the same bowl, add rice, vegetables, water, soy sauce and sesame oil and stir to combine.
5. Microwave on "High" for about 6-8 minutes.
6. Remove the bowl from microwave and immediately cover it for about 5 minutes.
7. Uncover the bowl and with a fork, fluff the rice.
8. Add in the cooked egg and gently stir to combine.
9. Garnish with green onion serve immediately.

Lentil Curry

Servings | 2   Time | 15 minutes
Nutritional Content (per serving):
Cal | 205   Fat | 4.2g   Protein | 12.6g   Carbs | 29.7g   Fibre | 15g

Ingredients:

- 360 millilitres (1½ cups) water
- 10 millilitres (2 teaspoons) olive oil
- 2½ grams (½ teaspoon) curry powder
- 15 millilitres (1 tablespoon) fresh lemon juice
- 105 grams (½ cup) split red lentils
- 2½ grams (½ teaspoon) ginger paste
- 1¼ grams (¼ teaspoon) red pepper flakes, crushed
- Salt, as required

Directions:

1. In a large glass microwave-safe bowl, add the water and lentils and microwave on "High" for about 14 minutes.
2. Remove the hot bowl from the microwave and stir well.
3. Cover the bowl and set aside.
4. In a microwave-safe bowl, add the oil and microwave for about 30 seconds.
5. Add the remaining ingredients except the lemon juice and microwave for about 1 minute, stirring once halfway through.
6. In the bowl of lentils, add the oil mixture and lemon juice and stir to combine.
7. Serve immediately.

Lentil & Rice with Veggies

Servings|6   Time|15 minutes
Nutritional Content (per serving):
Cal| 237   Fat| 2.1g   Protein| 7.4g   Carbs| 48.5g   Fibre| 5.2g

Ingredients:

- 1 (540-gram) (19-ounce) can ready-to-serve lentil soup
- 1 (255-gram) (9-ounce) package ready-to-serve brown rice
- Salt and ground black pepper, as required

- 1 (225-gram) (8-ounce) can mixed vegetables, drained
- 2 (115-grams) (4-ounce) cans diced roasted red peppers

Directions:

1. In a microwave-safe dish, add all the ingredients and mix well.
2. Cover the dish and microwave, covered on "High" for about 5-6 minutes.
3. Remove from the microwave and set aside, uncovered for about 1 minute before serving.

Beans & Corn Enchilada

Servings|6   Time|20 minutes
Nutritional Content (per serving):
Cal| 144   Fat| 1.4g   Protein| 6.1g   Carbs| 29.5g   Fibre| 5.9g

Ingredients:

- 200 grams (7 ounces) canned fire roasted tomatoes
- 200 grams (7 ounces) canned black beans, rinsed and drained
- 1¼ grams (¼ teaspoon) ground cumin
- 1¼ grams (¼ teaspoon) red chili powder
- 4 corn tortillas
- 165 grams (½ cup plus 2 tablespoons) salsa, divided
- 95 grams (¾ cup) corn
- 5 grams (2 tablespoons) fresh coriander, chopped
- 5 millilitres (1 teaspoon) fresh lime juice

Directions:

1. For enchilada sauce: place the canned tomatoes and 130 grams (½ cup) of salsa and mix well.
2. For filling: place remaining salsa and remaining ingredients except the tortillas in another bowl and mix well.
3. Arrange the tortillas onto a platter and top with the beans mixture.
4. Fold each tortilla over filling.
5. In the bottom of a large microwave-safe dish, spread ½ cup of the sauce.
6. Arrange the rolled tortillas over sauce and top with the remaining sauce.
7. Microwave on "High" for about 3-4 minutes.
8. Serve hot.

Pasta with Carrot Puree

Servings|1   Time|20 minutes
Nutritional Content (per serving):
Cal| 290   Fat| 2.4g   Protein| 13.8g   Carbs| 58.4g   Fibre| 11.8g

Ingredients:

- ❖ 120 millilitres (½ cup) water
- ❖ 75 grams (¼ cup) carrot puree
- ❖ 2½ grams (½ teaspoon) ground turmeric
- ❖ 20 grams (1 tablespoon) ketchup

- ❖ 100 grams (½ cup) pasta
- ❖ 10 grams (2 tablespoons) nutritional yeast
- ❖ 1¼ grams (¼ teaspoon) onion powder

Directions:

1. In a microwave-safe bowl, add the water and pasta and microwave on "High" for about 4 minutes, stirring once halfway through.
2. Remove from the microwave and stir in the remaining ingredients.
3. Microwave on "High" for about 2-3 minutes.
4. Remove from the microwave and stir in the ketchup.
5. Serve immediately.

Mac n Cheese

Servings | 1   Time | 10 minutes

Nutritional Content (per serving):

Cal| 384   Fat| 19.4g   Protein| 19.6g   Carbs| 32.1g   Fibre| 1.3g

Ingredients:

- ❖ 75 grams (½ cup) elbow macaroni
- ❖ 65 grams (½ cup) cheddar cheese, finely shredded
- ❖ 120 millilitres (½ cup) water
- ❖ Salt and ground black pepper, as required

Directions:

1. In an extra-large microwave-safe mug, add water and macaroni.
2. Arrange the mug on a large microwave-safe plate and microwave on "High" for about 2 minutes, stirring once halfway through.
3. Again, stir the macaroni and microwave on "High" for about 1-1½ minutes, stirring after every 20 seconds.
4. Remove the mug from microwave and immediately stir in cheese, salt and black pepper until melted.
5. Serve immediately.

Cauliflower Hummus

Servings|6   Time|25 minutes
Nutritional Content (per serving):
Cal| 140   Fat| 13.9g   Protein| 1.8g   Carbs| 4.1g   Fibre| 1.7g

Ingredients:

- 320 grams (3 cups) cauliflower florets
- 30 millilitres (2 tablespoons) water
- 3 whole garlic cloves, peeled
- 45 millilitres (3 tablespoons) fresh lemon juice
- Pinch of smoked paprika

- 75 millilitres (5 tablespoons) olive oil, divided
- 6¼ grams (1¼ teaspoons) salt, divided
- 30 grams (1½ tablespoons) tahini paste
- 15 millilitres (1 tablespoon) extra-virgin olive oil

Directions:

1. In a large microwave-safe bowl, mix together cauliflower, 30 millilitres (2 tablespoons) of oil, water, whole garlic cloves, and 2½ grams (½ teaspoon) of salt.
2. Microwave on "High" for about 15 minutes, stirring occasionally.
3. Transfer the cauliflower mixture into a high-speed blender and pulse until smooth.
4. Add remaining ingredients and pulse until smooth.
5. Transfer the hummus into a serving bowl.
6. Drizzle with extra-virgin olive oil and sprinkle with smoked paprika before serving.

Potato Chips

Servings | 5   Time | 20 minutes
Nutritional Content (per serving):
Cal | 144   Fat | 11g   Protein | 1g   Carbs | 11g   Fibre | 1g

Ingredients:

- ❖ 3 medium red potatoes, scrubbed and cut into thin slices
- ❖ Salt, as required

- ❖ 60 millilitres (¼ cup) olive oil
- ❖ 2½ grams (½ teaspoon) curry powder

Directions:

1. Line a large microwave-safe plate with paper towels.
2. In a large bowl, add all ingredients and toss to coat well.
3. Transfer the potato slices onto prepared plate in batches
4. Microwave on "High" for about 5-6 minutes, turning once in the middle way.
5. Repeat with the remaining slices.
6. Set aside for about 1-2 minutes before serving.

Plantain Chips

Servings|1   Time|20 minutes
Nutritional Content (per serving):
Cal| 261   Fat| 5.3g   Protein| 2.4g   Carbs| 57.8g   Fibre| 4.4g

Ingredients:

- ❖ Non-stick cooking spray
- ❖ 2½ grams (½ teaspoon) ground turmeric
- ❖ 5 grams (1 teaspoon) coconut oil, melted

- ❖ 1 plantain, peeled and sliced
- ❖ Salt, as required

Directions:

1. Grease a large microwave-safe bowl with cooking spray.
2. In a large bowl, add all ingredients and toss to coat well.
3. Transfer the half of plantain slices into the prepared microwave-safe bowl.
4. Microwave on "High" for about 3 minutes.
5. Now, set the microwave on "50% power" and microwave for about 2 minutes.
6. Repeat with the remaining plantain slices.
7. Serve warm.

Peanut Butter Cake

Servings|1   Time|10 minutes
Nutritional Content (per serving):
Cal| 368   Fat| 17.6g   Protein| 11.6g   Carbs| 44.8g   Fibre| 3.1g

Ingredients:

- ❖ 35 grams (¼ cup) plain flour
- ❖ 40 grams (2 tablespoons) smooth peanut butter
- ❖ 20 grams (1 tablespoon) maple syrup
- ❖ 1 gram (¼ teaspoon) baking powder
- ❖ 75 millilitres (5 tablespoons) unsweetened almond milk

Directions:

1. Add all the ingredients in a microwave-safe mug and mix until well combined.
2. Microwave on "High" for about 50-60 seconds.
3. Serve immediately.

Banana Cake

Servings|1   Time|10 minutes
Nutritional Content (per serving):
Cal| 382   Fat| 22.9g   Protein| 5.1g   Carbs| 45.3g   Fibre| 6g

Ingredients:

- 1 banana, peeled and mashed
- 2 grams (½ teaspoon) baking powder
- 2½ grams (½ teaspoon) ground cinnamon
- Pinch of salt
- 2½ millilitres (½ teaspoon) vanilla extract

- 20 grams (3 tablespoons) almond meal
- 10 grams (1 tablespoon) coconut sugar
- Pinch of ground ginger
- 15 grams (1 tablespoon) coconut oil, softened

Directions:

1. In a bowl, add all ingredients and mix until well combined.
2. Transfer the mixture into a microwave-safe mug.
3. Microwave on "High" for about 2 minutes.
4. Remove from microwave and set aside to cool for 5 minutes before serving.

Blueberry Cake

Servings | 2   Time | 10 minutes
Nutritional Content (per serving):
Cal | 400   Fat | 18.5g   Protein | 5.4g   Carbs | 54.3g   Fibre | 1.4g

Ingredients:

- 65 grams (½ cup) all-purpose flour
- Pinch of salt
- 60 grams (3 tablespoons) butter, melted
- 30 grams (2 tablespoons) plain Greek yogurt
- 35 grams (¼ cup) fresh blueberries

- 4 grams (1 teaspoon) baking powder
- 80 grams (¼ cup) granulated sugar
- 60 millilitres (¼ cup) milk
- 2½ millilitres (½ teaspoon) vanilla extract
- 5 grams (1 teaspoon) fresh lemon zest, finely grated

Directions:

1. In a bowl, mix together the flour, baking powder and salt.
2. In another bowl, add the sugar and butter and beat until smooth.
3. Add milk, yogurt and vanilla extract and beat until well combined.
4. Add the flour mixture and mix until just combined.
5. Fold in blueberries and lemon zest.
6. Divide the mixture in 2 microwave-safe mugs evenly.
7. Microwave on "High" for about 1½ minutes.
8. Remove from microwave and set aside to cool for 5 minutes before serving.

Chocolate Cake

Servings | 1   Time | 10 minutes
Nutritional Content (per serving):
Cal | 437   Fat | 38.9g   Protein | 10.8g   Carbs | 14.5g   Fibre | 3.2g

Ingredients:

- 15 grams (2 tablespoons) almond flour
- 40 grams (2 tablespoons) white sugar
- 45 grams (3 tablespoons) cream
- 1 egg
- Dash of vanilla extract

- 15 grams (1 tablespoon) unsweetened cocoa powder
- 15 grams (1 tablespoon) coconut oil, melted

Directions:

1. In a large microwave-safe mug, add all ingredients and mix until well combined.
2. Microwave on "High" for about 90-100 seconds.
3. Remove from microwave and set aside to cool for 5 minutes before serving.

Strawberry Tart

Servings|1   Time|10 minutes
Nutritional Content (per serving):
Cal| 338   Fat| 12.5g   Protein| 4.4g   Carbs| 51.9g   Fibre| 0.8g

Ingredients:

- ❖ Non-stick cooking spray
- ❖ 10 grams (1 tablespoon) icing sugar
- ❖ 35 grams (¼ cup) all-purpose flour
- ❖ 20 grams (1 tablespoon) butter, softened
- ❖ 30 millilitres (2 tablespoons) milk
- ❖ 20 grams (1 tablespoon) strawberry jam

Directions:

1. Grease a microwave-safe mug with cooking spray.
2. In a microwave-safe mug, mix together the butter and sugar.
3. Add the flour and milk and mix until well combined.
4. Make a well in the center of flour mixture.
5. Place the jam in the well.
6. With a spoon, gently smooth the batter over the jam evenly.
7. Microwave on "High" for about 45-60 seconds.
8. Remove the mug from microwave and set aside to cool before serving.

Apple Crisp

Servings|1   Time|15 minutes
Nutritional Content (per serving):
Cal| 459   Fat| 30.2g   Protein| 3.8g   Carbs| 46.9g   Fibre| 3.8g

Ingredients:

For Filling:

- ❖ 1 apple, peeled, cored and thinly sliced
- ❖ 10 grams (½ tablespoon) butter, melted
- ❖ 2½ grams (1 teaspoon) all-purpose flour
- ❖ 5 grams (1 teaspoon) brown sugar
- ❖ 1¼ grams (¼ teaspoon) ground cinnamon

For Topping:

- ❖ 20 grams (3 tablespoons) rolled oats
- ❖ 10 grams (1 tablespoon) all-purpose flour
- ❖ 10 grams (1 tablespoon) brown sugar
- ❖ 1¼ grams (¼ teaspoon) ground cinnamon
- ❖ 40 grams (2 tablespoons) butter, softened

Directions:

1. For filling: in a bowl, add apple slices and remaining ingredients and toss to coat well.
2. For topping: in another bowl, add oats, flour, brown sugar and cinnamon and mix well.
3. With a pastry blender, cut in the butter until a crumb like mixture forms.
4. In a microwave-safe bowl, arrange half of apple slices and top with half of topping mixture.
5. Repeat the layers.
6. Microwave on "High" for about 3 minutes.
7. Remove from the microwave and serve warm.

Pumpkin Cookies

Servings | 10   Time | 15 minutes
Nutritional Content (per serving):
Cal | 160   Fat | 13g   Protein | 0.8g   Carbs | 12.6g   Fibre | 1.7g

Ingredients:

- 55 grams (¼ cup) pumpkin puree
- 60 grams (1/3 cup) almond butter
- 2½ millilitres (½ teaspoon) vanilla extract
- 5 grams (1 teaspoon) pumpkin pie spice
- 75 grams (1/3 cup) coconut oil
- 120 grams (1/3 cup) honey
- 200 grams (2 cups) unsweetened coconut, shredded

Directions:

1. Line a large cookie sheet with parchment paper. Set aside.
2. In a large microwave-safe bowl, mix together all ingredients except coconut.
3. Microwave on "High" for about 20 seconds.
4. Add shredded coconut and stir to combine well.
5. With a tablespoon, place the mixture onto prepared cookie sheet in a single layer.
6. Refrigerate for at least 2 hours to set completely.

Chocolate Chips Bread Pudding

Servings|2   Time|15 minutes
Nutritional Content (per serving):
Cal| 326   Fat| 14.5g   Protein| 8.3g   Carbs| 42.8g   Fibre| 2.8g

Ingredients:

- ❖ 2 Hawaiian sweet rolls, halved
- ❖ 90 millilitres (1/3 cup) milk
- ❖ 1 egg
- ❖ ¾ gram (1/8 teaspoon) ground cinnamon
- ❖ 20 grams (2 tablespoons) semi-sweet chocolate chips
- ❖ 20 grams (1 tablespoon) unsalted butter, softened
- ❖ 40 grams (2 tablespoons) white sugar
- ❖ 1¼ grams (¼ teaspoon) vanilla extract
- ❖ Pinch of ground nutmeg

Directions:

1. Spread a thin layer of each onto Hawaiian roll half.
2. Then cut each half into 4 cubes.
3. In a small bowl, add the milk, egg, sugar, cinnamon and vanilla and whisk until well combined.
4. In a large microwave-safe ramekin, place the roll cubes and chocolate chips and mix.
5. Place the egg mixture over the top evenly and with a fork, gently stir to blend.
6. Sprinkle the top of with nutmeg.
7. Microwave on "High" for about 1 minute.
8. Remove the ramekin from microwave and with a fork, stir the mixture.
9. Microwave on "High" for about 45 seconds.
10. Remove the ramekin from microwave and with a fork, stir the mixture.
11. Microwave on "High" for about 75 seconds, stirring after every 15 seconds.
12. Remove from the microwave and serve warm.

Printed in Great Britain
by Amazon